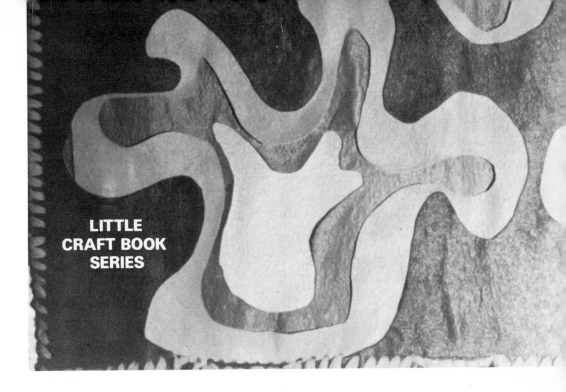

**LITTLE
CRAFT BOOK
SERIES**

APPLIQUÉ & REVERSE APPLIQUÉ

By JO IPPOLITO CHRISTENSEN
& SONIE SHAPIRO ASHNER

STERLING
PUBLISHING CO., INC. **NEW YORK**

Oak Tree Press Co., Ltd.
London & Sydney

Little Craft Book Series

Aluminum and Copper Tooling
Animating Films without a Camera
Appliqué and Reverse Appliqué
Balsa Wood Modelling
Bargello Stitchery
Beads Plus Macramé
Beauty Recipes from Natural Foods
Big-Knot Macramé
Candle-Making
Cellophane Creations
Ceramics by Slab
Coloring Papers
Corn-Husk Crafts
Corrugated Carton Crafting
Costumes from Crepe Paper
Crafting with Nature's Materials
Creating from Remnants
Creating Silver Jewelry with Beads
Creating with Beads
Creating with Burlap
Creating with Flexible Foam
Creating with Sheet Plastic
Creative Lace-Making with Thread and Yarn
Cross Stitchery

Curling, Coiling and Quilling
Decoupage—Simple and Sophisticated
Embossing of Metal (Repoussage)
Enamel without Heat
Felt Crafting
Finger Weaving: Indian Braiding
Flower Pressing
Folding Table Napkins
Games You Can Build Yourself
Greeting Cards You Can Make
Hooked and Knotted Rugs
Horseshoe-Nail Crafting
How to Add Designer Touches to Your Wardrobe
Ideas for Collage
Junk Sculpture
Lacquer and Crackle
Leathercrafting
Macramé
Make Your Own Elegant Jewelry
Making Paper Flowers
Making Picture Frames
Making Shell Flowers
Masks

Metal and Wire Sculpture
Model Boat Building
Monster Masks
Nail Sculpture
Needlepoint Simplified
Net-Making and Knotting
Off-Loom Weaving
Organic Jewelry You Can Make
Patchwork and Other Quilting
Pictures without a Camera
Potato Printing
Puppet-Making
Repoussage
Scissorscraft
Scrimshaw
Sculpturing with Wax
Sewing without a Pattern
Starting with Stained Glass
Stone Grinding and Polishing
String Things You Can Create
Tissue Paper Creations
Tole Painting
Trapunto: Decorative Quilting
Whittling and Wood Carving

Dedicated to our children, Lisa Renee Ashner, Stuart Alan Ashner, and Peter John Christensen, and in memory of Elizabeth Kirsten Christensen.

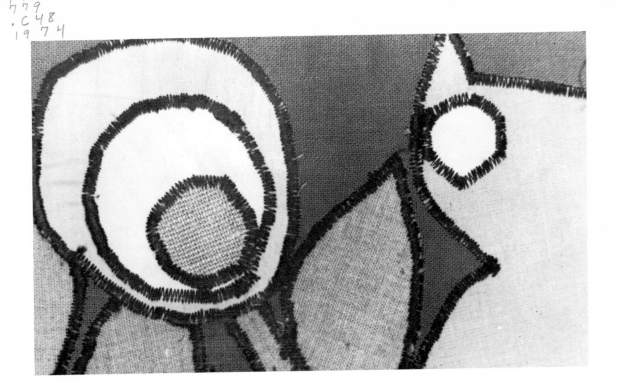

Contents

Before You Begin

Essentially, appliqué is the applying of one fabric to another in order to form a design. Traditionally, this meant hand sewing smaller pieces of fabric onto either larger pieces of fabric or onto garments.

In today's world of zig-zag sewing machines, iron-on fabric bonding agents, and fabric glue, much of the traditional hand sewing has been eliminated. And, you can appliqué to decorate a new item or as an afterthought, to cover a stain or tear. Projects in this book follow this new trend as well as the traditional one.

In choosing fabrics for appliqué, consider that felt, vinyl, and double knits do not ravel, and, therefore, you will not need to turn under the cut edges. In other instances, when you do have to turn under the edges, select a light-weight fabric to avoid bulk.

If your garment or background fabric is washable, choose washable trims for appliqué. For example, if you sew a felt appliqué onto a cotton dress, the dress will have to be dry cleaned.

Some sewing shops sell bags full of scraps. Remnants often provide just what you need to complete a lovely appliqué item. Anyone you know who sews (if you do not sew yourself) probably has a wealth of good scraps for appliqué.

The tools you need for appliqué depend on which methods you choose. As a result, no general list is given here from which you can gather your equipment. Instead, the book is arranged by technique, and each section includes a discussion of what materials you need.

The only thing you should always be equipped with is creativity—your own. The rest is arbitrary and changeable. Use your imagination.

Appliqué with Glue

Fabric and glue can be the main tools for appliqué, especially for a beginner. The technique is quite simple, but the results can be really unusual.

Torn-Felt Picture

You can tear multi-colored felt scraps to create interesting shapes and a feathery edge. Pull the felt apart with your hands or with a pair of pliers. Pull all edges, so you do not let a single cut edge remain.

Arrange several pieces of feathered felt on a sheet of paper in a design you like. Spread glue or paste on the backs of the torn-felt pieces. Then place a large piece of felt over the odd-shaped pieces. This will be the background. Press in place. Turn the whole thing over. Carefully peel the paper off. Even a child will delight in doing this.

Finish by mounting your creation on stiff cardboard or Masonite (pressed board). Frame if you wish. See Illus. 31 for an example of torn-felt appliqué.

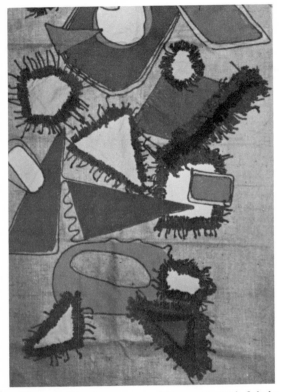

Illus. 1 and 2 are examples of an abstract in yarn and fabric on burlap. Glue the fabric pieces you choose in place with a glue made especially for fabric. (Most fabric glues come in tubes.) Glue the yarn on by first squeezing a line of glue where you want the yarn, and then by pressing the yarn over it.

Illus. 1. This is one possible yarn and fabric abstract you can make. Use your imagination to create interesting designs.

Yarn Pictures

You might also enjoy making a yarn picture. Follow the same directions as for the torn-felt picture, or lay lines of glue on the background fabric and press pieces of different colored yarn over the glue.

Illus. 2. Close-up of the abstract in Illus. 1.

Illus. 3. This thematic mural was done by a group of individuals: each person created one rectangle. The separate creations were then sewn together to complete the project.

A mural, like the one in Illus. 3, is a good project for a group of friends or classmates. Each person makes a drawing of a scene. The drawings can all have the same theme (underwater is the theme here) or not. Then transfer the drawings to pieces of fabric (burlap was used here), using dressmaker's carbon (follow the manufacturer's directions).

On this mural, each design was entirely executed in yarn and glue by its creator. Then the rectangles were sewn together on the machine.

A fabric border was sewn around the rectangles to give a finished look.

Fabric Creations

You may wish to reproduce in fabric a drawing you have made. The drawing does not have to be intricate to make an effective appliqué. First trace the drawing, then cut up the tracing and use it as a pattern. Cut the large portions of your drawing out of fabric. Glue the fabric in place on a background fabric with glue made especially for fabric. Apply the glue with a brush. Reproduce any lines with yarn or other trimmings, and glue them in place. You can then either frame your appliqué or attach a dowel by which to hang it.

To make the dowel attachment, first turn under the edges of the background fabric $\frac{1}{4}$ inch (6 mm.). Stitch by machine. Turn the edges under once more—this time one inch (25 mm.). Stitch by hand. Leave the ends of the top hem open. Slip a dowel rod through the hem. The dowel should be 3 or 4 inches (7.5 or 10 cm.) longer than your wall hanging is wide. Hang the picture by a piece of matching yarn that you tie to both ends.

Simple shapes make excellent subjects for a beginner's appliqué picture. Illus. 28 and 30 were cut from fabric scraps and glued in place.

Re-create the view out of your window, a painting, or a photograph. Illus. 29 is an example of a fabric painting. To give the illusion of background and foreground, glue one piece of fabric (sky color) to the entire piece of Masonite that will be your picture. Then, for example, glue the mountains on, from the top line to the bottom of the picture, over the portion of sky that you do not want to show. Begin the foothills next and then the foreground, following the above procedure. Place the building and the trees on top of it all.

Glue each layer in place as before, using a brush and glue made especially for fabric. Frame after the picture has dried thoroughly.

Appliqué Shower Curtain

Decorating a vinyl shower curtain (see Illus. 46) can be fun and the finished product will certainly perk up your bathroom.

Choose an over-all design for the best effect. Draw your own or re-create and enlarge the one in Illus. 46 by the grid method, described on page 29, or by using a pantograph (available in art supply shops). This method is easier if you have a large (8 foot × 8 foot or 2.4 m. × 2.4 m. minimum) linoleum floor. (The standard shower curtain is 6 feet × 6 feet or 1.8 m. × 1.8 m.). You must have a sheet of paper large enough, but you may tape the pieces together. Follow the directions included with your pantograph to enlarge the design.

When you have your design enlarged, you are ready to begin the appliqué part. On your diagram, number every part. Mark each piece with the color you want to use.

Make a pattern from each numbered section on the drawing. Trace each piece, using tracing paper and a black felt-tipped pen. Then add a $\frac{1}{4}$ to $\frac{3}{8}$ inch (1 cm.) seam allowance on the sides, which you will tuck under another piece (see Illus. 4).

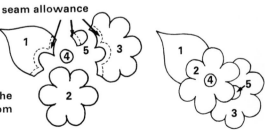

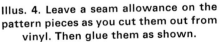

Illus. 4. Leave a seam allowance on the pattern pieces as you cut them out from vinyl. Then glue them as shown.

7

Cut around each pattern piece. To cut them out of vinyl, place the *right* side of the vinyl down on a table. Arrange the pattern pieces *right* side down on top of the vinyl. Move the pieces around to get the optimum use out of your vinyl. Trace around each pattern piece with a felt-tipped pen. Number each piece *as you go*. Check and double check the numbers and colors. Also be sure that you place each pattern piece face down. Cut out all the pieces.

Lay the large design on the floor. Put each piece in its place on top of the paper. Using an adhesive that will stick vinyl to vinyl, glue the overlapping pieces together. All but two or three pieces should be attached to each other. Roll the paper and vinyl up together very carefully.

Lay a purchased vinyl shower curtain on the floor. On top of that, unroll the paper with the design drawn on it and the vinyl pieces on it. Then slip the paper out. You will need two other people to help you.

Carefully position the vinyl pieces on the shower curtain. Then glue them in place.

Do not forget to put on your initials and the date.

Your shower curtain is now ready for compliments.

Appliqué with Contact Paper

The clothes hamper in Illus. 5 shows a quick way to decorate a store-bought item so that it fits into your décor. A very simple silhouette in contact paper works best.

Draw your design on paper. Cut round it and place it on the wrong side of a piece of contact paper. Trace it; cut it out. Pull off the backing and stick the contact to a hamper, wastebasket, or other object. In Illus. 5, the bunny's tail is a ball made from ball fringe that you can purchase by the yard from sewing supply shops. It is glued in place.

Illus. 5. Appliquéing with contact paper, as was done on this clothes hamper, is a simple way to decorate an otherwise plain item.

Appliqué with Plastic Tape

Plastic or vinyl tape is a good, quick, yet durable way to decorate any plastic or vinyl object. A solid-colored director's chair (Illus. 6) takes on a new look even when you only apply two colors of tape in only two widths.

Using colored strips of paper, arrange your design on a sheet of paper the same size and color as your chair seat and back. Tape or glue your final placement of the stripes in place. (Be sure to use glue made especially for glueing vinyl.) Number each stripe so you will know in which order to place them on your chair.

To apply the design to your chair, open the chair up completely. Put the tape on, following your diagram. *Do not stretch the tape.* Measure to be sure that your lines will be parallel.

Illus. 6. Plastic-tape appliqué is one way to make your vinyl director's chair different from all others.

Iron-On Appliqué

An unusual but very effective appliqué technique is to use an iron-on bonding material, available in sewing supply shops, to fuse your appliqués to the background. If you buy bonding material which has no backing, pin it directly to the fabric. Then pin the pattern in place over this and cut both at the same time. If your bonding material has a paper backing, you simply draw or trace the appliqué onto the paper backing of the bonding material and then cut out the appliqué and the iron-on bonding *at the same* *time* (so they will be exactly the same size). Then simply iron, following the manufacturer's directions.

Using this iron-on material helps you produce neat, smooth appliqué work. In addition, it saves you from having to turn under and clip the edges of your appliqué and it prevents the edges from ravelling, even if you do not stitch over them. It also means that you do not have to baste the appliqués in place, but that they will not slip before you can sew them securely.

Machine Stitching
with Iron-On Appliqués

Machine stitching after applying an iron-on fabric bonding agent serves several purposes. First of all, you increase durability. This is especially important on garments or items which will receive lots of wear or handling.

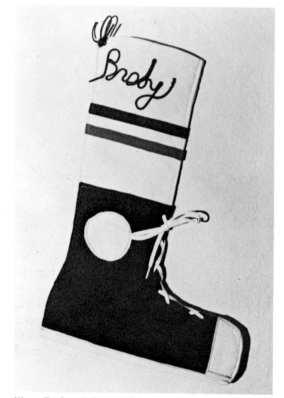

Illus. 7. Straight machine stitching accents the iron-on appliqué on this decorative stocking.

Even though you do machine stitching, you should still use the iron-on bonding agent, because it prevents puckering and stretching of the appliquéd pieces of fabric, as well as of the background fabric.

All machine stitches should be medium width, zig-zag stitches set so close together that they resemble the Satin stitch in embroidery (see Illus. 48). (You may use straight stitching when a zig-zag would not be appropriate, as in Illus. 7.)

Apply any design you wish to a garment or household item that you have bought or made. It is easier to put an appliqué design on the pocket of a ready-made dress if you remove the pocket first.

Baby Quilt

The baby quilt shown in Illus. 13 is a good example of machine-stitched iron-on appliqué. The various appliqués which adorn the patchwork squares were first fused onto the squares with iron-on bonding. To do this, first cut as many squares as you wish, of whatever sizes you choose (the patches here were all either 2 inches, 4 inches, or 8 inches—5, 10 or 20 cm.), making sure to leave an extra $\frac{1}{4}$-inch (6-mm.) seam allowance. You can use remnants of permanent-press cottons, broadcloth or kettlecloth, as was done for this quilt, or whatever fabrics you choose. Also, consider using pieces of partially worn-out baby sheets as backgrounds or for the appliqués (the Raggedy Ann and Andy were cut from an old sheet).

Illus. 8. Close-up of the baby quilt. Besides being decorative, this quilt can be educational as well. Notice the C for car and the A for apple, Ann and Andy, for instance.

Next, cut decorative appliqués from different fabrics—to add a variety of textures to your quilt—and from the bonding agent at the same time (so they will be exactly the same size). Iron the appliqués to the squares, following the directions that come with the iron-on material.

Then machine embroider the appliqués. To create padded stitching, as was done for this quilt, first place a strand of thread along the edge of the appliqué and then do a very close zig-zag stitch (this will look like a Satin stitch) over the thread. You could also do this by hand, by placing two strands of embroidery floss along the edges, couching or tacking the strands down every inch (25 mm.) or so and then doing the Satin stitch with two strands of embroidery floss over the laid threads (see Illus. 48 for the Satin stitch).

When all your appliqué work is finished, sew together the squares. Then, finish the quilt. First choose a complementary colored fabric for the backing. Cut it several inches (4 or 5 cm.) larger than the patchwork side. With the right sides together, sew round the edges of the quilt top and bottom, leaving a space so you can turn the quilt right-side-out. Stitch this opening closed by hand. You can sew on a ruffle by hand, if you wish. Then place yarn ties in various squares as instructed on page 32. (For a heavier weight quilt, you can add cotton batting. See directions on page 31.)

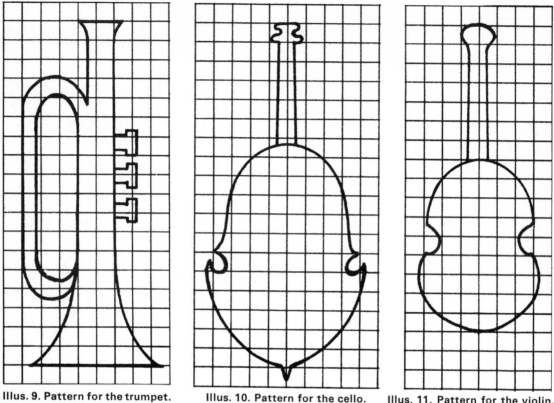

Illus. 9. Pattern for the trumpet.   **Illus. 10. Pattern for the cello.**   **Illus. 11. Pattern for the violin.**

Musical Skirt

If you are particularly fond of music, or if you play an instrument, why not make a musical skirt like the one in Illus. 12, using the iron-on bonding?

First, buy a pattern for a long, A-line skirt without a front seam and cut it out from a washable, permanent-press fabric. Be sure to determine the proper length before you cut the skirt out, and leave only a small amount for the hem, so it will not be too obvious. Sew the darts, the back seam, and put in the zipper.

Next, decide what instruments you want to use. For the skirt in Illus. 12, a trumpet, cello, tuba, banjo and two violins adorned each side (see Illus. 9 to 11, 14 and 15). You can either use scraps of material you already have, or you can buy some especially for this project. You need

12

Arrange the instruments attractively on the skirt front and back and carefully iron them in place. After they are securely fused to the skirt, zig-zag around each instrument on the machine.

Complete the skirt, following the pattern's instructions.

about 12 to 18 inches ($\frac{1}{3}$ to $\frac{1}{2}$ metre) of fabric for each instrument. Place the bonding material under the fabric and cut the instruments and the bonding material out together. You need about $2\frac{1}{2}$ yards (2 metres) of 18-inch (45-cm.) wide bonding material for this skirt. Pin the instrument patterns securely to ensure that you cut both exactly the same size.

Illus. 13. A wonderful way to stimulate Baby and Mother is a multi-colored, many patterned appliquéd baby quilt such as this one.

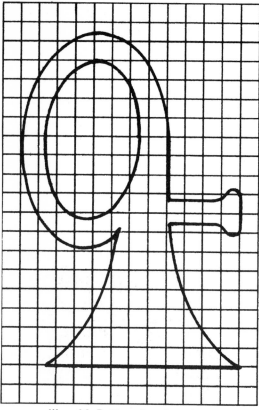

Illus. 14. Pattern for the tuba.

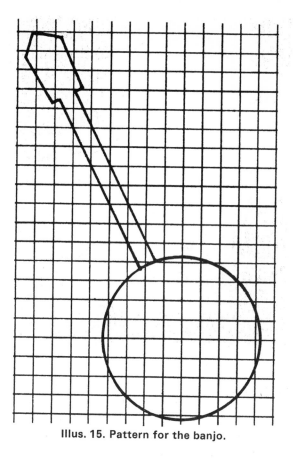

Illus. 15. Pattern for the banjo.

Barbecue Apron

A good idea for a present for a father or grand-father would be an apron, like the one shown in Illus. 17, with the handprints of his children or grandchildren. You could even embroider the names and possibly the birthdates of the relatives on the hands.

To make the apron shown, you need a 24-inch (60-cm.) long piece of a machine-washable, 45-inch (110-cm.) wide material (this apron is made from kettlecloth), several pieces of print fabric, about $1\frac{1}{4}$ yards (1 metre) of iron-on bonding material, 5 yards (4.5 metres) of double-fold bias tape and a piece of interfacing (stiffener) 7×20 inches (17.5×50 cm.) to line the back of the pocket. The finished apron shown is 20×38 inches (50×95 cm.), but you can make

14

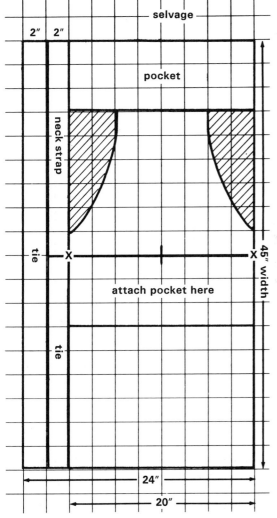

selvage

2" 2"

pocket

neck strap

tie X———————————————X 45" width

attach pocket here

tie

|← 24" →|

|← 20" →|

Illus. 16. Pattern for the barbecue apron. The cross-hatched area is the only waste if you use 45-inch (110-cm.) wide material. Attach ties at the X's.

yours any length shorter than this, using the remainder of the 45-inch (110-cm.) width of material (7 inches or 17.5 cm. here) for a pocket.

To make the apron, first cut it out following the pattern in Illus. 16. Then, on the piece of interfacing 7 × 20 inches (17.5 × 50 cm.), write in script, "Can I give you a hand?" Trace over your writing with a dark, indelible marking pen, so that the ink shows up on the reverse side. Now, go over the letters on this reverse side, so that you can use them as a lettering guide. Sew the interfacing to the pocket you cut, using the bias tape to bind the edges of the two fabrics together.

Release the drop feed mechanism from your machine to enable the material to glide in any direction so that you can embroider on your machine. Using an embroidery hoop, set your machine on zig-zag and use the machine to achieve the Satin stitch. (If your machine does not have a zig-zag attachment, you can, of course, do this embroidery by hand. If you plan to hand embroider the pocket, you can write on the pocket with pencil. You should still use the interfacing behind the pocket, as it gives extra body to it.)

The lettering on the reverse side of the interfacing is your guide. Be sure to check the tension of your thread to see how it looks, as the right side is face down.

After you embroider, you can also sew a small hand to the pocket, if you wish. Then sew the pocket to the apron along the side edges, 3 inches (7.5 cm.) below the curves as shown in Illus. 18. Sew an inch (2.5 cm.) reinforcement in the middle of the pocket as shown in Illus. 18. After the pocket is in place, sew the bias tape around the

Illus. 17. A fashionable and practical use for your appliqué is a barbecue apron such as this colorful one.

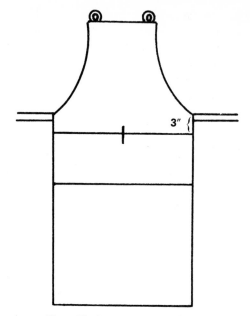

Illus. 18. Apron construction.

entire apron. Just place the tape over the raw edges of the fabric and stitch. This adds color to the apron and also prevents the edges from ravelling.

Next, trace the hands of family members or friends. Cut paper patterns for each hand and place them on top of some iron-on bonding material and whatever decorative fabrics you have chosen. Cut hands from both materials at the same time. Keep the pieces pinned together until you iron them, because if the iron-on material slips from underneath the print fabrics, it sticks to the iron.

Arrange the various hands on the apron before you iron them on. Some of the hands may overlap for a more interesting composition. Iron and then zig-zag the pieces on the machine to secure them in place.

After the hands are in place, sew on the ties and the neck strap as follows: From the remaining 4 × 45-inch (10 × 110-cm.) piece of fabric (see Illus. 16), cut two strips. From the end of one of the strips, cut 23 inches (57 cm.), as shown in

Illus. 16, for the neck strap. Leaving only a $\frac{1}{4}$-inch (6-mm.) seam allowance, fold the right sides of this strip together and sew into a tube. Turn right-side-out. To make fastening loops (see Illus. 19), cut two pieces from this tube, each 3 inches (7.5 cm.) long. Place these loops at the edges of the top of the apron as shown in Illus. 19. Sew securely so that the neck strap ends can go through the loops.

Sew the ends of the remaining 17-inch (42-cm.) tube. Wrap one end of this neck strap around one of the loops and sew securely (see Illus. 19). At the end of the loose end, sew a small piece of velcro

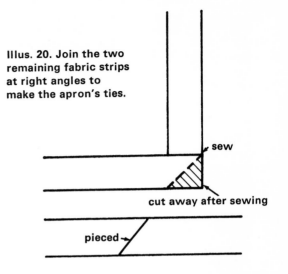

Illus. 20. Join the two remaining fabric strips at right angles to make the apron's ties.

sew

cut away after sewing

pieced

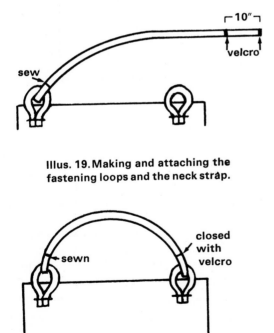

r 10" ┐

velcro

sew

Illus. 19. Making and attaching the fastening loops and the neck strap.

closed with velcro

sewn

(the material that adheres to itself) to fit the width of the strap. Sew another piece of velcro 10 inches (25 cm.) from the end of the strap (see Illus. 19). To fasten the apron, put the strap through the loop. When the pieces of velcro meet and adhere to each other, the strap will close. If this positioning is not correct for the wearer, then move the velcro so that the apron fits comfortably.

To make the two ties for the apron, take the remaining two 2-inch (5-cm.) wide strips of fabric and put them together at right angles as shown in Illus. 20. Sew them together on a diagonal and cut away the excess material. You now have one long strip. Make into a tube, as you did for the neck strap, and turn. Cut the tube in the middle—you have two ties. Sew the ties to the apron just below the curve as shown in Illus. 18.

All that remains is for you to plan a barbecue—the apron is ready to use.

Wall Hangings

The wall hangings in Illus. 21 and 32 and on the back cover all begin with two large pieces of background fabric that are the same size. You appliqué the design (first by iron, then by machine) to the first, and use the second as a lining.

To line the checkerboard in Illus. 21, for instance, place the right sides together. Stitch on the machine, leaving a $\frac{1}{2}$-inch (12-mm.) seam allowance, around the two bottom corners, up both sides (to within one inch—25 mm.—of the top), and across the top (see Illus. 22). Secure the seam allowance at the openings you have made by hand stitching.

Trim the corners. Turn and press. Stitch the bottom by hand. Press again. Stitch across the top, through both thicknesses, one inch (25 mm.) from the top.

Stain a wooden dowel rod. Slip it through the hole you have made for it on top. Attach a leather

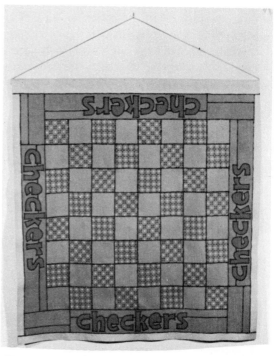

Illus. 21. You can use this functional wall hanging on a table or the floor—to play checkers!

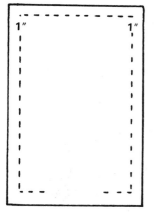

Illus. 22. Construction of the checkerboard wall hanging.

Illus. 23. Close-up of the checkerboard hanging. Notice how the machine stitching emphasizes the ironed-on letters.

thong, yarn, wire, or other string-like filament to the ends of the dowel for a hanger.

You may finish the bottom as you did the top, if you wish, or you may make the bottom edge a little fancier, as in the banner on the back cover. To do this, follow the instructions for finishing Illus. 21 with one exception: do not stitch round the bottom corners. Make a separate pattern for the points. Cut out two pieces exactly alike from your background fabric. Stitch, with a $\frac{3}{8}$-inch (1-cm.) seam allowance, and trim the excess fabric as shown in Illus. 25. Turn and press.

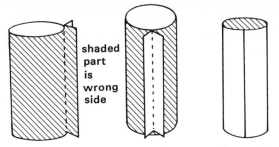

Illus. 26. To make hanging tabs, sew and press as shown, with the seam in the middle of the strip.

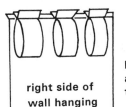

Illus. 27. Pin the tabs as shown on top of the right side.

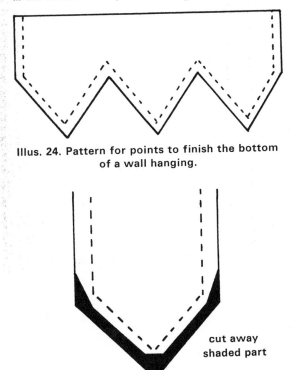

Illus. 24. Pattern for points to finish the bottom of a wall hanging.

Illus. 25.

Stitch both thicknesses of the piece with the points to the front piece of the wall hanging, right sides together. Press the seam up. Lay your wall hanging flat on a table, front side down. Tuck under the remaining raw edge and stitch by hand. Press.

To finish the top as in Illus. 32, cut several strips of fabric twice as wide as you want them plus one inch (25 mm.) for seam allowances. Cut them long enough to go up and over a dowel rod and back to the wall hanging. Again, add one inch (25 mm.) for seam allowances.

Stitch, right sides together, along the long edge, making a $\frac{1}{2}$-inch (12-mm.) seam allowance. Press the seam open. Turn so that the seam is in the middle of the strip and not along one edge (see Illus. 26). Press. Fold the strip in half so that the

Illus. 28. Simple shapes cut from felt make an effective and attractive appliqué, as you can see in "Sunset."

Illus. 29. Try "painting" with fabric, as was done here. Any scenic view is an interesting possibility for an appliqué.

Illus. 30. Even a child can make an appliqué picture. All he or she need do is cut a particular shape from fabrics, and glue the pieces onto a board.

20

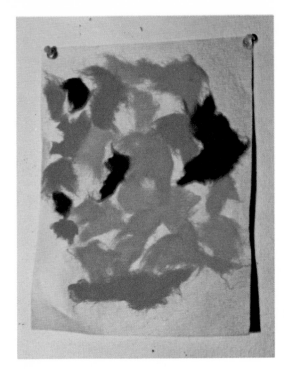

Illus. 31. You can achieve unusual, colorful effects if you tear pieces of felt from a larger piece. Notice the feathery texture which results.

Illus. 32. There is no limit to the variety of wall hangings you can create using appliqués. This is one which may inspire some ideas of your own.

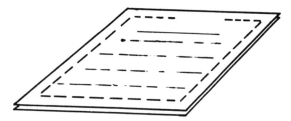

Illus. 33. Construction of the wall hanging. Stitch four corners and three sides by machine, turn, press, and stitch the last side by hand.

fabric with a pencil and cut the fabric out. Place the pieces on a piece of background fabric also 6 × 9 inches (15 × 22 cm.). With a large needle and thread, baste the pieces together just enough

raw edges meet. Be sure that the seam is on the inside. Pin together as shown in Illus. 27. Placing right sides together, now put the lining on top of the wall hanging and strips. Stitch all four corners and three sides (see Illus. 33), with a $\frac{1}{2}$-inch (12-mm.) seam allowance. Trim the corners, turn and press. Stitch the fourth side by hand. Press. Hang by a dowel rod.

Machine-Stitched Appliqué with Basting

Skirt

Sometimes it is helpful to baste your appliqué pieces in place before machine stitching them. This was done on the skirt in Illus. 38. To make this unusual skirt, draw a series of designs on paper measuring 6 × 9 inches (15 × 22 cm.). Then, advance to fabric. Cut up the drawings so that you have patterns by which to cut the fabric pieces. Simply trace round the patterns onto the

Illus. 34. Front of the appliquéd skirt. Each square, individually executed, was first basted together, and then machine sewn.

to hold until you stitch by machine. If several crafters have donated their drawings to this project, you may mark each one's name with fabric paint, which comes in tubes. You can also use this paint for design details.

At this point, someone must secure the pieces to the background fabric with a machine-sewn zig-zag stitch. In this skirt, the co-ordinator inserted black strips of fabric between each square, and between groups of squares. You can use more or fewer of these strips to adjust the skirt to fit.

Finish the skirt with a hem and waistband.

Play Rug

A good thing to keep at grandma's house, or just to have for playing with, is a play rug like the

Illus. 35. One of the appliquéd panels on the skirt shown in Illus. 34 and 38.

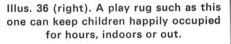

Illus. 36 (right). A play rug such as this one can keep children happily occupied for hours, indoors or out.

Illus. 37 (left). You can transform an old (or new) work shirt into a truly unique cover-up with appliqués.

Illus. 38 (right). As many people as are available can contribute to a joint project, such as this colorful skirt.

Illus. 39 (left). Directions for the flowers on this spring-like work shirt begin on page 40.

Illus. 40. Although traditional molas (reverse appliqué) are made from layers whose edges are stitched under, this one, made from felt, is simply glued in place.

Illus. 41. Molas are not only wall hangings. This tote bag, for instance, was also made using the reverse appliqué technique.

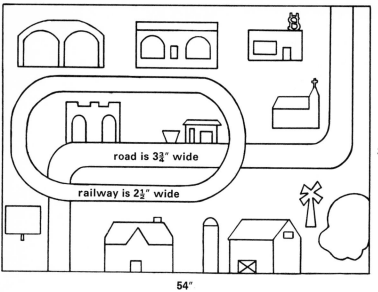

Illus. 42. Pattern for the play rug. Follow this to make patterns for the buildings shown in Illus. 36.

road is 3¾" wide

railway is 2½" wide

36"

54"

one in Illus. 36. This rug depicts a home, farm, pond, church, bank, warehouse, airport, gas (petrol) station, fire house, highway and railway. It is meant to be used with small cars, trains, planes, boats and dolls.

The size of the rug was determined by the width of the materials used. Because felt and naugahyde (imitation leather) come 54 inches (135 cm.) wide, it is easiest to purchase a yard (metre) of each in green for the base. Neither of these fabrics ravel, so you do not need to hem them or turn under the edges and stitch.

The appliquéd parts of the rug are felt. Many fabric shops sell felt in 12-inch (30-cm.) squares. Buy various colors, such as light blue, navy, tan, white, black and red.

Procedure

Following Illus. 42, make patterns for the buildings. Then cut the pattern pieces from felt. Sew or glue any small parts to the buildings to which they belong. Embroider the names on the buildings and decorate the cut-outs with embroidery floss, using the Outline or Satin stitch (see Illus. 48)—fish go in the pond, flowers and shrubs around the house, details on the barn, silo, and warehouse. The hose of the gas pump is the end of a shoe lace, sewn so that the lace comes from the pump. On the end of the lace, sew a small piece of velcro so that the pump can be replaced after the cars are filled. The fire house has a real bell.

26

Notice that the road breaks for the railway track. You can easily construct a bridge from two 4-inch (10-cm.) squares of wood or stiff plastic foam as shown in Illus. 43. Cut one block diagonally to form the approach. Cut the other out in the middle to make a tunnel for the railway to go through. The road is $3\frac{3}{4}$ inches (9 cm.) wide and the railway track is $2\frac{1}{2}$ inches (6 cm.) wide. Use felt or seam binding for the rails and sew them on top of the track before you sew it to the rug.

After you have cut out all the buildings and other parts, baste them in place on the felt. Then sew them by machine so they will stay permanently. Leave the bottoms of the hangar doors unstitched, so that planes can be parked under (or inside) them. You can turn one row of buildings upside-down, if you wish, to face the outside edge of the rug, so that if two children want to play, one can sit on each side of the rug.

After all the parts are sewn on, place the wrong

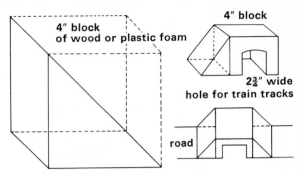

Illus. 43. Pattern for the bridge.

side of the felt and naugahyde together and sew round the edges. You may pink the edges, if you wish.

On the back of the naugahyde, about 4 inches (10 cm.) from one edge, and in the middle of the fabric, sew a shoe lace. When the rug is finished, you can then roll it up, wrap the lace around it, and tie it closed.

Hand-Stitched Appliqué

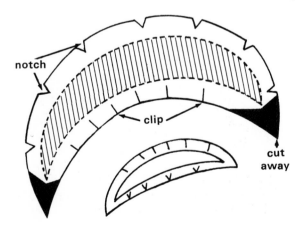

Traditional, hand-stitched appliqué is shown on the napkins in the bottom right corner of the front cover. To make napkins, cut out a very simple design from fabric you have chosen, leaving an extra $\frac{1}{4}$ inch (6 mm.) for the seam allowance. Press the seam allowance under. You will have to clip and notch the fabric to make the curves lie flat (see Illus. 44). Pin or baste your motif in place on whatever fabric you choose for the napkins. Hand stitch in place with blind stitches. Blind

Illus. 44. Clip and notch curved pattern pieces. Then insert a cardboard pattern the shape of the pattern and press round it. Remove to stitch.

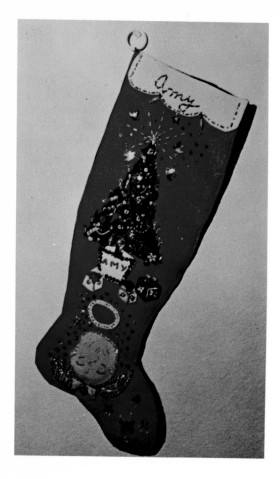

Illus. 45. This personalized stocking is a good example of the versatility of hand-stitched appliqué.

Illus. 46. Now you can even be creative in your bathroom. Try making a decorative shower curtain like this one using vinyl and glue.

stitches are very tiny stitches with which you connect the turned-under seam allowance of your appliqué to the background. The stitches should be invisible from the top.

The Christmas stocking in Illus. 45 is stitched just like the napkins with one exception: you stuff each fabric area with polyester fibre just before securing it to your background. The three-dimensional effect you achieve in this way is called Trapunto. Then add whatever other decorative designs you wish.

Mural

You can enlarge any original drawing or design in order to make it into a mural. A third grade class made the mural in Illus. 47. One child's drawing (voted on by the class) was enlarged by the grid method. Draw a $\frac{1}{2}$-inch grid (criss-crossed lines $\frac{1}{2}$ inch—12 mm.—apart) over the design you plan to enlarge. On another piece of paper, draw a one-inch (25-mm.) grid (criss-crossed lines one inch—25 mm.—apart) with the same number of squares. Copy the portion of the drawing in each of the small squares into each of the corresponding large squares. In this way, using these dimensions, you double the size of the original drawing. By changing the size of both grids, you can vary the size of your final design. To reduce the size, simply reverse the process.

Once your chosen drawing is the size you want it, transfer it to a background fabric (burlap or hessian was used here). Place dressmaker's carbon between the design and the background fabric and trace the design. This helps you in placing your fabric pieces later.

You may then cut up the paper drawing to use as a pattern for cutting out your appliqué pieces.

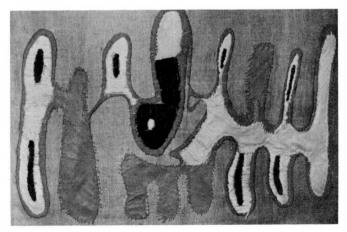

Illus. 47. Hand-stitched appliqué need not be minute nor intricate, as you can see by the stitching on this mural.

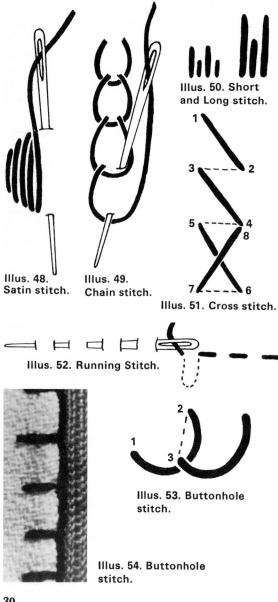

Illus. 48.
Satin stitch.

Illus. 49.
Chain stitch.

Illus. 50. Short
and Long stitch.

Illus. 51. Cross stitch.

Illus. 52. Running Stitch.

Illus. 53. Buttonhole
stitch.

Illus. 54. Buttonhole
stitch.

Attach the fabric pieces to the background with a Satin stitch (see Illus. 48).

Other decorative stitches you can use to appliqué the design pieces onto the background are the Buttonhole stitch (see Illus. 53 and 54), the Running stitch (Illus. 52), the Chain stitch (Illus. 49), the Cross stitch (Illus. 51), and the Short and Long stitch (Illus. 50).

Quilt

Decorative hand stitching becomes the main attraction in another manner in the quilt in Illus. 58. With odd-shaped fabric scraps and just three pretty stitches, you can make something useful out of nothing.

Your fabric pieces need not be any particular size or shape, nor do they need to fit together perfectly. You may wish to sew the odd-shaped pieces within a set form, such as squares as shown in Illus. 58, but this is not necessary.

Choose a piece of light-weight fabric for the background. Its color does not matter since it will not show. The background fabric should be the size you would like your finished quilt to be, minus the width of the ruffle and plus $\frac{5}{8}$-inch (15-mm.) seam allowances on all four sides. Piece the background if necessary.

Starting in one corner, lay your quilt pieces onto the background fabric one by one. Baste each piece in place before going on to the next one. Turn under the raw edges $\frac{3}{8}$ inch (1 cm.), as shown in Illus. 55. Press each piece as you go.

You may do decorative stitching as you go, or

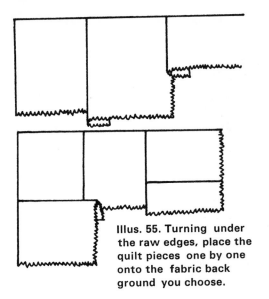

Illus. 55. Turning under the raw edges, place the quilt pieces one by one onto the fabric back ground you choose.

you may wait until you have sewn all of your scraps on. Use a wooden, screw-type embroidery hoop when you sew. Be sure to catch the backing fabric with your stitches to provide more stability and durability for your quilt. See Illus. 56 and 57 for stitch suggestions.

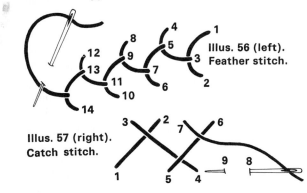

Illus. 56 (left). Feather stitch.

Illus. 57 (right). Catch stitch.

After you have attached all of your quilt pieces to the background fabric, and have sewn the decorative stitches, begin working on the ruffle and lining. Cut the ruffle twice as deep as you would like it to be when it is finished and two or three times the circumference of the quilt. Add $1\frac{1}{4}$ inch (3 cm.) for seam allowances. Sew the ends together. Fold the ruffle in half lengthwise. Press. To gather the ruffle, sew a basting stitch (beginning at the seam) round the entire top edge (not the folded edge), leaving 6 to 8 inches (15 to 20 cm.) of thread at the beginning and end. Gently pull these threads so that the ruffle gathers. Pull until the ruffle is the same circumference as the quilt. Be sure to distribute the gathers evenly along the entire length.

Now attach the ruffle to the quilt. To do this, place the ruffle on top of the right side of the quilt all the way round. Stitch the ruffle and quilt together on the machine, making sure you sew below the basting stitches so they do not show. Turn the ruffle out, and, from the back, press the seam towards the middle.

For warmth, you can insert an old blanket or quilt batting (available at sewing supply shops) at this point. Lay the quilt, face down, on a large table. Place the batting, which comes in strips, on top. Overlap the strips carefully, so the whole inside of the quilt is covered. Choose a lining (or backing) of a durable fabric. Cut a piece that is several inches (25 mm.) larger than the quilt on each side. Place the lining, right side up, on top of the batting. Baste through all layers along the edges. Turn the quilt over.

With a needle and thread whose color complements your quilt, take a stitch, in the middle of

Illus. 58. One of the most traditional uses of appliqué is on quilts. This patchwork quilt is just one of the many types you can make.

the quilt, through all the layers. Bring the needle back to the top close to the first stitch. Tie the thread ends in a square knot on the right side of the quilt (Illus. 59). Working out towards the edges, place more such ties at random or follow any pattern you like. Keep the lining as smooth as possible. When you have finished the tying, turn the quilt over. Trim the batting to the gathering stitch of the ruffle. Trim the lining to one inch (25 mm.) beyond that gathering line. Turn that

one-inch (25-mm.) hem under and hand stitch the lining to the ruffle, hiding the gathering stitches. Press. Your quilt is ready to use.

Bell Pull

Mementoes from a trip are often thrown into drawers and forgotten. A trip to Africa resulted in the bell pull in Illus. 60. A bell pull fits hard-to-decorate, long, narrow walls such as between two doors or in an entrance hall. Needlepoint makes the effective background onto which bush jacket patches were appliquéd.

Bargello is needlepoint that is composed of vertical stitches. In this bell pull, the Bargello stitches which surround the patches were turned $90°$ to become horizontal stitches. This brings the viewer's eye to the patches.

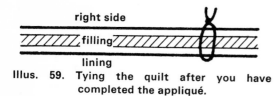

Illus. 59. Tying the quilt after you have completed the appliqué.

The background for all needlepoint is called canvas. It is best to do Bargello on Mono 14 (14 threads or mesh to the inch) canvas. The new interlocked Mono canvas is recommended as the interwoven threads are more durable. This also makes it more difficult to distort the canvas threads and enables you to cover the canvas more evenly.

Use graph paper of the same size as the canvas you will use (14 squares per inch) to work out your design. You may use the design pictured in Illus. 60, or create your own.

Cut the canvas the length and width that you want plus a 1½-inch (4-cm.) margin on each side (you will use the margin later for blocking). Bind the edges of the canvas with masking tape. If you use a bell pull hanger which you have bought, plan the width of the bell pull to fit the hanger. (The average width is 7 inches—17.5 cm.) Stitch four mesh beyond the hardware measurement (still following the pattern), so that you can turn under the worked area as the hem of the bell pull.

Use three strands of 2-ply Persian yarn and a size 20 blunt-end tapestry needle for the Bargello stitches. The yarn for the Bargello stitch can be 20 to 22 inches (50 to 55 cm.) long; however, for the Continental stitch, it should only be 18 inches (45 cm.) long, as the rough canvas wears the yarn thin. Never make knots in needlepoint. Instead, leave about a one-inch (25-mm.) tail of yarn on the wrong side. Cover this with your stitches as you work. To end the yarn, simply run it under the stitches that you have already worked—on the wrong side.

The design here is over four mesh (four threads). The second stitch in the line is a two-mesh step

from the first stitch. By placing more than one stitch on each step, you form an arc pattern. This 4 : 2 pattern is easy to follow. Once you have established the line pattern, you need only drop

Illus. 60. One section of the bell pull. The combination of appliqué and Bargello makes this an especially unusual project.

33

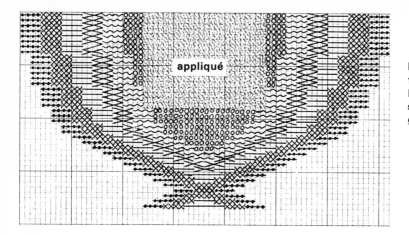

appliqué

Illus. 61. Bargello line pattern for the bell pull. Although this bell pull was done in rust, red, shades of orange and shades of green, you can use this pattern with any colors you wish.

four mesh below the preceding stitch. Share the whole with the stitch above.

You can actually stitch vertically by simply turning the canvas. When you hang the bell pull, the stitches will be horizontal.

Using two strands of 4-ply Persian yarn, work the lettering and the area immediately surrounding it (see Illus. 63) in the Continental stitch (see Illus. 62). Make up your own alphabet on graph paper or follow the one in Illus. 63.

Leave the canvas blank in the areas where your appliqué designs will go.

Because your piece of needlepoint is probably not out of shape very much, you do not need to block it to re-set the starch. Instead, simply place the bell pull between two damp terry-cloth towels and press.

After the bell pull has dried, sew on the patches by hand. Be sure that the needlepoint canvas does not show around your appliqué. If it does show, you can add a few compensating stitches after you have sewn the patches in place.

After you have attached the patches, zig-zag, on the sewing machine, the edge of the canvas outside the last row of needlepoint. Trim the canvas. Turn back the edge of the needlepoint so that at least two to four mesh of worked canvas are part of the hem. Then, turn back the top edge of the bell pull about $1\frac{1}{2}$ inches (4 cm.) to make a casing for the hanging hardware (see Illus. 64).

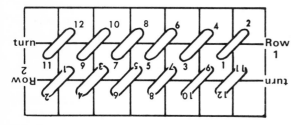

Illus. 62. Continental stitch.

The type of hardware used for the bell pull in Illus. 60 consists of a round metal rod which fits into the decorative wooden moulding as shown in Illus. 64. Notice in Illus. 65 that another piece of moulding was attached to the bottom of the bell pull to weigh it down and ensure that it hangs evenly. You can, of course, use any type of hanging mechanism you wish for your bell pull; various types are available in hardware stores, and in sewing and needlecraft shops.

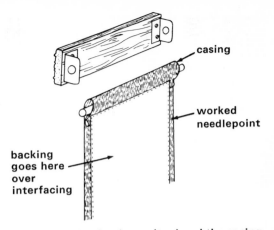

Illus. 64. Hanging hardware (top) and the casing you make to attach it.

Illus. 63. Close-up of the bell pull. Follow the lettering here or make up your own alphabet.

Turn under the raw edges of the casing you have made, and stitch it down by hand (see Illus. 64). Also turn under 1½ inches (4 cm.) at the bottom edge and stitch under the raw edge.

Now apply iron-on interfacing to the back of the canvas to give it added body and to help the needlepoint retain its blocked shape. To apply the interfacing, place the needlepoint face-down on a terry-cloth towel so you do not flatten the stitches when you iron.

Choose an appropriate fabric for a backing, such as corduroy or cotton velvet. Turn under the raw edges of the fabric backing. With the right sides facing out, blind stitch the backing fabric to the needlepoint.

To finish the edge of the bell pull, either crochet a chain using four full strands of Persian yarn (12 strands of 2-ply Persian yarn), or buy and attach some sort of attractive edging. If you

35

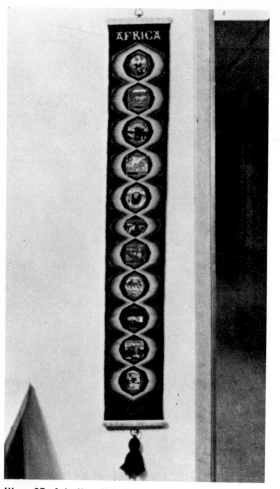

AFRICA

Illus. 65. A bell pull is just the thing to fill up an elongated, empty spot on your wall.

crochet a chain, lay it *wrong side up* along the edge and hand stitch it in place. Insert the hanging hardware and hang.

Child's Work Shirt

A cheery work shirt, like the one shown in Illus. 37, is convenient to use as a shirt, jacket, or beach robe. To make one, purchase a long-sleeved, denim work shirt (an outgrown long-sleeved boy's shirt will do, as long as it is a solid color). If the wearer of the shirt is short, you may cut off and hem the tails of the shirt. Be sure the shirt—and all the appliqués you use—are permanent press and washable.

Also buy 4 yards (3.5 metres) of pre-gathered lace, or enough to go around the edges of the bottom, front placket, cuffs and collar. Place the lace under the edges of the shirt and stitch, either by hand or machine. Most work shirts come with top stitching, so machine stitching looks very much in place.

On scraps of permanent-press cotton or a cotton/dacron blend, trace the clowns' patterns pieces in Illus. 66 to 70. The patterns for the feet and trousers are the same for both clowns except that the length is increased for the tall clown (the shaded areas in Illus. 67 and 68 show how much you need to increase). Cut *two* of each pattern piece so that you can stuff the clowns with polyester fibre filling before you sew them to the shirt.

To construct the various clown parts, place the right sides of the two cut-out pieces together. Sew, leaving only a $\frac{1}{4}$-inch (6-mm.) seam allowance. Make sure also to leave open those sections indicated in the various diagrams for ease in stuffing. Stuff each pattern part, but not too much—just enough to give the bodies three-dimensional forms. After you have stuffed each piece, turn under the open edges and sew.

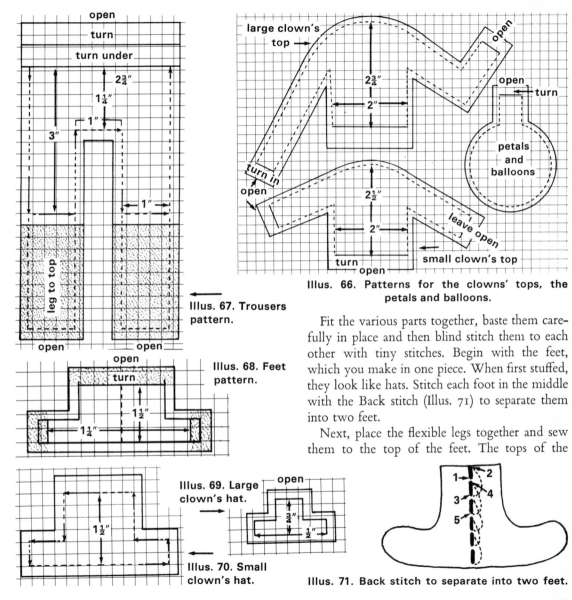

open
turn
turn under
$2\frac{3}{4}''$
$1\frac{1}{4}''$
$1''$
$3''$
$1''$
leg to top
open   open

Illus. 67. Trousers pattern.

large clown's top →
open
$2\frac{3}{4}''$
$2''$
open
turn
petals and balloons
turn in
open
$2\frac{1}{2}''$
$2''$
leave open
turn
open
small clown's top

Illus. 66. Patterns for the clowns' tops, the petals and balloons.

open
turn
$1\frac{1}{2}''$
$1\frac{1}{4}''$

Illus. 68. Feet pattern.

Illus. 69. Large clown's hat.

$1\frac{1}{2}''$

open
$\frac{3}{4}''$
$\frac{1}{2}''$

Illus. 70. Small clown's hat.

Fit the various parts together, baste them carefully in place and then blind stitch them to each other with tiny stitches. Begin with the feet, which you make in one piece. When first stuffed, they look like hats. Stitch each foot in the middle with the Back stitch (Illus. 71) to separate them into two feet.

Next, place the flexible legs together and sew them to the top of the feet. The tops of the

1→ 2
3   4
5

Illus. 71. Back stitch to separate into two feet.

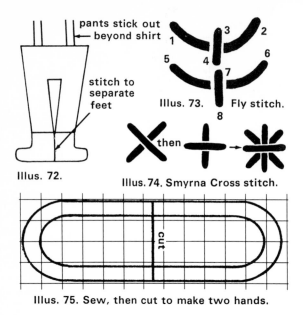

pants stick out
← beyond shirt

stitch to
separate
feet

Illus. 72.

Illus. 73. Fly stitch.

X then ✝ → ✳
Illus. 74. Smyrna Cross stitch.

Illus. 75. Sew, then cut to make two hands.

cut

trousers extend beyond the shirt width. Just sew the extra width to the back side of the trousers. Tuck the shirts into the trousers. You may stitch suspenders (braces) to the top of the shirt first. On the short clown, seam binding was used for the suspenders; on the tall clown, rick-rack was used.

Make both hands in one piece: sew completely around the oval pattern piece that comprises the hands (Illus. 75) and then cut in the middle to make two hands. Place the stuffed hands inside the shirt. Before you sew the clowns' hands, first sew the rick-rack strings of the balloons onto the work shirt (the shirt shown has seven balloons). Position the rick-rack so the hands will fit over it. Because the stuffed arms are flexible, and can be moved slightly, it will look as if the clowns are holding onto the strings.

Use some left-over lace from the work shirt's edging, gather it some more, and shape it into a circle to place it as the collar by sewing the front inside edge of the circle to the clown's shirt.

Now embroider the clowns' faces. Both have the same face, but the features are embroidered differently. The cheeks, eyes and nose of the short clown (which is to go on the shirt's back) were embroidered with the Satin stitch. The mouth was embroidered in the Fly stitch (see Illus. 73). For the tall clown (on the shirt's front), the Chain stitch was used for the nose and cheeks, the Fly stitch was used for the mouth and Cross stitches were used for the eyes (see Illus. 74).

Next, place the head over the hole of the lace circle and sew it to the collar and the top of the shirt (see Illus. 76).

To make the short clown's hair, wrap cotton or acrylic yarn round four fingers about six times. Mark the middle of the yarn and stitch on the machine, making sure the yarn lays flat. Stitch this middle seam (it forms the part in the hair) to

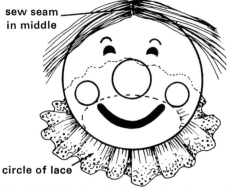

sew seam
in middle

circle of lace

Illus. 76. Tall clown's head, placed on a circle of lace.

38

Illus. 77. Run a thread through the middle of a strand of yarn to help keep the hair neat.

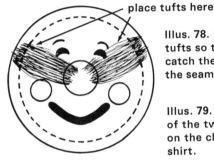

place tufts here

Illus. 78. Place hair tufts so that you catch the ends in the seam.

Illus. 79. Close-up of the two clowns on the child's work shirt.

the top of the stuffed clown head (see Illus. 78). You may run a thread through the yarn hair as shown in Illus. 77 to keep the hair manageable. If you sew the thread through the middle of each strand of yarn, the thread will not show. Put the stuffed hat over the top of the hair.

For the tall clown's hair, make two separate tufts of hair by wrapping yarn around three fingers five times. Place the tufts where shown in Illus. 78 so that you can catch the ends in the seam when you sew the head (the top of the head is bald). Set the small hat on top of the head (at the bald part) between the tufts of hair.

Now pin the clowns to the work shirt, baste them in place and then sew to the shirt with blind stitches.

In the hand of the short clown that does not have the balloons, you can sew a couple of flowers cut from a commercial strip of machine-embroid- ered appliqué. Sew the flowers onto the shirt and then place the hand to look as if the clown is holding the flowers. You can also sew a flower behind the hat of the tall clown.

To complete the work shirt, you can embroider the child's name on the pocket, if you wish. It is easier to do this if you remove the pocket first.

To wash the shirt, turn the buttoned shirt inside out. Wash in warm water on a gentle cycle or follow the instructions on the shirt. If your wash- ing machine does not have a gentle cycle, either wash by hand or in the machine inside a pillow case or bag. Machine dry.

Flowered Work Shirt

To make a flowered work shirt like the one in Illus. 39, use a shirt with an out-dated collar or purchase a denim work shirt in the men's department. If the sleeves are too long, you can alter them as follows: Take off the button and turn the cuff up. Place lace behind the edge of the cuff and stitch it down. Replace the button on the opposite side of the cuff—it will still button. Instead of the lace's being on the bottom edge, towards your fingers, it is behind the folded cuff. You may stitch the cuff in the folded position, if you wish (see Illus. 80).

Also sew lace around the collar and down the front placket.

The appliqués on this shirt are made and sewn on very much like those for the clown shirt on page 36. First, you need two of each pattern piece. Because the parts are small, it is easier to place the right sides of the fabric together, and then trace all the patterns in Illus. 83 on the top piece of fabric (on the back side). (See below for specific construction directions for the pattern pieces.) Do *not* cut before you sew.

Stitch, leaving a $\frac{1}{4}$-inch (6-mm.) seam allowance. Cut the pieces out just prior to stuffing them so that you do not misplace any. Turn and stuff the pieces just enough to give them body. Do not fill them too full or they will stand out too much from the shirt and also make the shirt too stiff and heavy.

Procedure

In making the flowers from printed fabrics, choose the side of the petals or leaves that is most attractive—with small prints, you can get different patterns on the two sides of each petal or leaf.

Make two flowers with petal A, the small round petal in Illus. 83. Cut seven petals for each flower. Stitch, cut out, turn and stuff the petals. Sew the bottom of the turned and stuffed petals closed. Take a doubled thread and stitch through the flowers so that the petals form a circle (see Illus. 81). Close the circle and reinforce it by going round through the petals in the circle again.

Then make the corollas or central parts. One

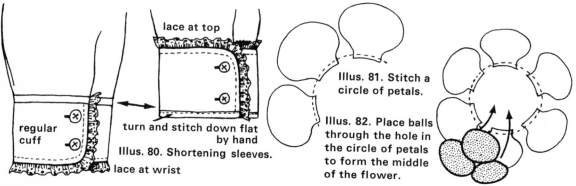

regular cuff

lace at top

turn and stitch down flat by hand
Illus. 80. Shortening sleeves.
lace at wrist

Illus. 81. Stitch a circle of petals.

Illus. 82. Place balls through the hole in the circle of petals to form the middle of the flower.

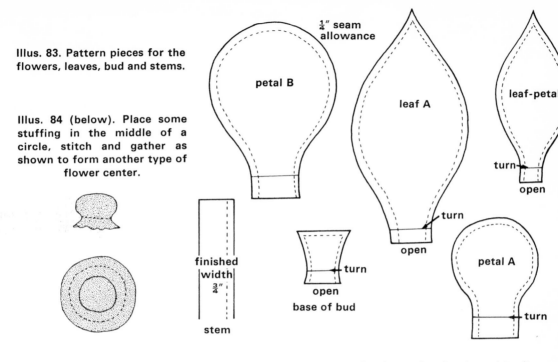

Illus. 83. Pattern pieces for the flowers, leaves, bud and stems.

Illus. 84 (below). Place some stuffing in the middle of a circle, stitch and gather as shown to form another type of flower center.

$\frac{1}{4}''$ seam allowance

petal B

leaf A

leaf-petal

turn

open

turn

open

finished width $\frac{3}{4}''$

stem

turn

open

base of bud

petal A

turn

way is to take balls from commercial ball fringe (those on the flowers on this shirt were one inch —25 mm.— in diameter) and the braid connecting them. Stuff the braid through the holes in the middle of the circle of the flowers. Secure the braid on the backs of the flowers (see Illus. 82).

Now make a flower from the leaf-petal pattern in Illus. 83. Make eight petals. Turn and stuff. Sew the bottoms closed. Make the same type circle as for the previous flowers. Take one-inch (25-mm.) diameter ball fringe and place it through the middle of the circle of petals. Secure in place.

For the flower on the right in Illus. 39, make five petals from the pattern for petal B in Illus. 83.

Cut a circle, about $1\frac{1}{2}$ inches (4 cm.) in diameter, for the middle of the flower from another piece of fabric (see Illus. 84). Place a small piece of stuffing in the middle of the fabric and gather the material by stitching a small circle. Secure this in the middle of the circle of petals, as you did for the previous flowers.

To make the doughnut-shaped flower in the middle in Illus. 39, take an 8 × 3 inch (20 × 7.5 cm.) strip of fabric and make a tube by putting the right sides of the fabric together. Leaving a small seam allowance, sew and turn. Stuff and sew the tube in a circle, making a doughnut shape. From a $1\frac{1}{2}$-inch (4-cm.) diameter circle of fabric,

41

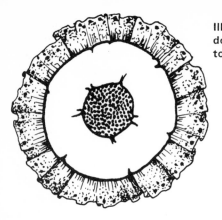

Illus. 85. Completed doughnut flower sewn to a circle of lace.

2½" ---------------------------------- fold and sew

leave open to slip in bottom of pot

Illus. 86. Pattern for the small flower pot.

3½"

cut two

3"

5½"

1"

3½"

finished pot

2½"

make a fabric hub as you did for the previous flower. Place this in the middle of the doughnut and secure.

From a remnant of old-fashioned-type lace, cut about an 8-inch (20-cm.) strip and gather it into a circle (the lace used was 2 inches—5 cm.—wide). Sew the doughnut shape to the lace.

Now draw around the patterns for the leaves (Illus. 83), sew and then cut out. Stuff. For variety, you can use two different fabrics for the front and back of the leaf. Instead of having the seam on the side of the leaf, place the seam down the middle so that the leaf is two tones (see Illus. 87). Take a few stitches in the leaves after stuffing

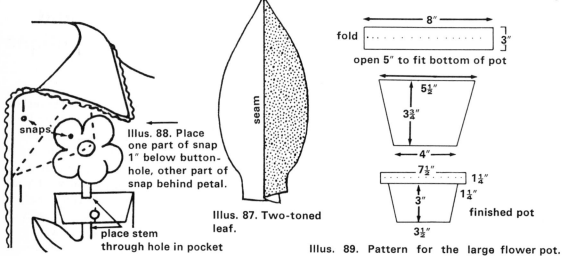

snaps

Illus. 88. Place one part of snap 1" below button-hole, other part of snap behind petal.

place stem through hole in pocket

seam

Illus. 87. Two-toned leaf.

8"

fold

3"

open 5" to fit bottom of pot

5½"

3¾"

4"

7½"

1¼"

3"

1¼"

finished pot

3½"

Illus. 89. Pattern for the large flower pot.

fold and sew the two short sides and the open side, making sure to leave an opening in the middle to slip in the base of the flower pot. Turn under the $\frac{1}{4}$-inch (6-mm.) seam allowance and stitch down (you can baste this) so that the edge of the opening is smooth.

Cut the pot base from two pieces of fabric. Leave a small space in the top seam to stuff. Stuff the base and top of pot. Slip the base into the slit you left open in the bottom of the pot top so there is about $\frac{1}{2}$-inch (12-mm.) overlap at the top. Sew securely. If you plan to zig-zag the pot and stems to the shirt (you can hand sew them), all you have to do is baste the parts together since you eventually zig-zag over this joining. Make sure you do not stuff the pots too full.

Illus. 90. Close-up of the flower on the front of the shirt.

them to help condense the extra fullness caused by the curved shape of the seam.

Make stems from rick-rack or a tube you make by sewing a length of material so that the finished stem is about $\frac{3}{4}$ inch (2 cm.) wide (see Illus. 83). (This stem can fit through the hole in the shirt pocket that workmen use for a pencil.) Baste, then stitch the flowers, stems and leaves to the shirt. Then make buds from the same fabrics as the flowers. Draw two petals from the leaf-petal pattern in Illus. 83. Sew and stuff. Sew the two petals, overlapping, and attach the bottom green base of the bud (see Illus. 83). Sew onto the stems.

The flowers grow from pots; one small (Illus. 86) and one large (Illus. 89) (the only difference is size). To make the pots, cut rectangles of fabric,

Combination Hand- and Machine-Stitched Appliqué

Learn-To Book

By combining hand- and machine-stitched appliqué, you can make a "learn-to" book for a child (see Illus. 96). This is a good, educational toy to occupy a child at home, while waiting at a doctor's office, or when travelling, for example.

First decide how many pages you want your book to contain. Choose a sturdy fabric, such as sailcloth, for the pages themselves. The pages of the book illustrated here are $8\frac{1}{2}$ inches wide by 9 inches (21 × 22.5 cm.) high. Since sailcloth is

43

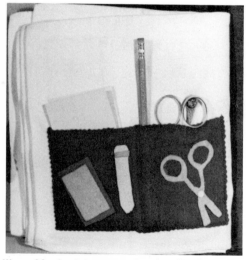

Illus. 91. For every four pages, cut a piece of sailcloth as shown.

usually 36 inches (90 cm.) wide, this is a convenient page size. For every four pages of the book, cut a piece of sailcloth 10 inches (25 cm.) tall (see Illus. 91).

Now, plan how you want to decorate the pages to best help your child become acquainted with a variety of skills. Illus. 94 shows some ideas you may incorporate in your book: buckling, distinguishing left and right hands, counting, lacing shoes, and distinguishing shapes. You might like

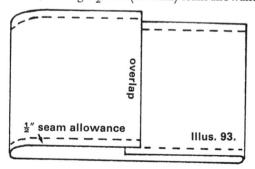

Illus. 92. Activity page in the "learn-to" book.

to include an activity page (Illus. 92) for storing paper, pencils, crayons, and a pair of scissors (unless your child is too young for scissors).

Work mostly with felt and vinyl which are not only decorative, but are also easy to work with, because they do not ravel. Use pinking or scalloping shears to decorate the edges. Incorporate as many other materials as you can into your pages for educational purposes. The clock in Illus. 95, for example, utilizes several different types of materials. You can cut the hands from a plastic lid, and connect them to the book with a metal brad (spread fastener) so they are free to turn. Be sure to place a small piece of plastic underneath the hands, so the brad does not wear through the fabric. On the clock in Illus. 95, the brad is in the middle of a machine-made buttonhole.

After you have decided upon your appliqués, and have carefully sewn or glued them, four pages abreast as shown in Illus. 91, to the top side of your 36 inch by 10 inch (90 × 25 cm.) piece of sailcloth, you are ready to complete the book itself. With the right side up, fold the two outside pages towards the middle, overlapping slightly in the middle (see Illus. 93). Stitch along the top and bottom, leaving a $\frac{1}{2}$-inch (12-mm.) seam allowance

overlap

$\frac{1}{2}$" seam allowance

Illus. 93.

Illus. 94. Various pages in the "learn-to" book. Think up some other ideas for pages which will educate a child.

Illus. 95 (below). A moveable clock can help a child learn to tell time.

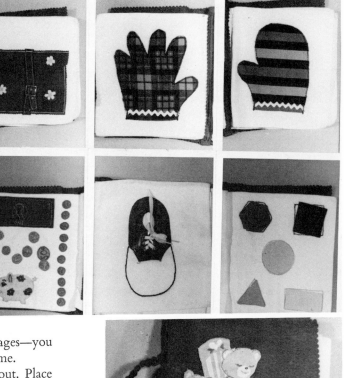

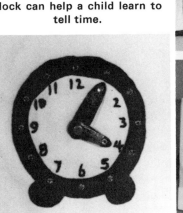

as shown. Repeat this for all of your pages—you will be working with four pages at a time.

Carefully turn the pages right side out. Place on a terry-cloth towel, and press the seams flat. Do not try to press the entire page because the activities are back to back and wrinkles might appear.

When all of your pages are stitched and pressed, stack them one on top of the other. Stitch them together by hand, with Back stitches down the middle of the book.

To make the covers for the book, cut and decorate a piece of felt, with pinking shears, at least $18\frac{1}{2}$ inches wide by $10\frac{1}{2}$ inches (46×26 cm.) high.

Illus. 96. Appliqué a juvenile design and embroider the child's name on the book's cover for a finishing touch.

45

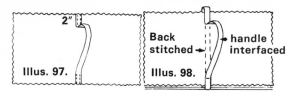

2"

Illus. 97.

Back
stitched → ↔ handle
interfaced

Illus. 98.

For the book's closure, cut a double thickness of felt, with pinking shears, 1 inch by 3 inches (25 × 75 mm.). Using heavy duty thread, sew this piece of felt to the middle of the front cover, so that it overlaps the edge about ½ inch (12 mm.) (see Illus. 96). Sew a heavy duty snap for the closure on the felt strip and on the back cover.

If you wish, you can sew on a pinked piece of felt, about 4 inches by 5 inches (10 × 12.5 cm.) or any size you have available, on the inside of the back cover to serve as a litter bag.

To make a handle, cut two felt strips with pinking shears, each 1 inch by 12 inches (2.5 × 30 cm.). Cut a piece of interfacing slightly narrower than these straps to keep the handle from stretching and tearing. Cut and pink another strip of felt 1 inch wide and approximately 10½ inches (2.5 × 26 cm.) long (the height of the cover) which will serve as the inside spine of the book. Machine stitch the handle with the interfacing between the two thicknesses of felt. Stitch as close to the edge as possible.

Place the handle on the outside of the cover and sew down 2 inches (5 cm.) of the handle at the top and bottom of the cover (see Illus. 97). Since the handle is 12 inches (30 cm.) long and the cover only 10½ inches (26 cm.) long, there is adequate room for your child to slip his or her hand under the handle to carry the book easily (see Illus. 97).

At the same time that you sew the handle to the outside, you may attach the inside spine, which you have already cut and pinked, to the cover. If your machine will take the thickness of the felt, you can machine-stitch the spine down for about ½ inch (12 mm.) on the inside of the cover, top and bottom, at the same time you stitch the handle down. If your machine will not accommodate the thickness of the felt, after you have sewn the handle on, sew down ½ inch (12 mm.) at each end of the spine by hand, using a Back stitch and heavy duty thread.

Slip the stacked pages of the book under the spine. By hand, Back stitch the pages to the cover close to both edges of the spine (see Illus. 98). Be careful not to catch the handle when sewing. Stitch a second time.

Your book is now ready for your child to use.

Molas (Reverse Appliqué)

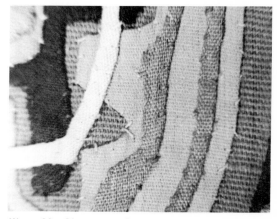

Illus. 99. Close-up of a mola. Notice the tiny stitches which hold the edges of the upper layers under.

46

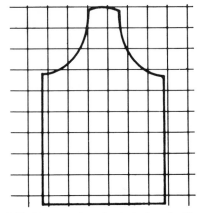
Illus. 100. Pattern for the tote bag in Illus. 41.

The mola was originally developed by the natives (Cuna tribesmen) of San Blas, a collection of 360 islands off the Caribbean coast of Panama. (The two molas on the front cover, from the collections of Anna Lee Rubin and Gloria Berenson, came from that area.)

The actual origin of the folk art is hazy, but it is speculated that when early Spanish priests insisted that the women's bodies be clothed, they invented the mola.

The mola is most often used on blouses, although Central Americans do make wall hangings for tourists.

The technique is actually reverse appliqué. You place several layers of different colored fabric one on top of the other, and then cut away these layers in a planned, yet unwritten, design to reveal the fabrics on the lower levels. You then carefully turn under the raw edges and stitch them by hand (see Illus. 99).

A fourth grade class made the mola in Illus. 40 from felt. Because felt does not ravel, the students did not need to turn under the edges and stitch. Instead, they simply glued the layers in place.

The layers themselves are held together on the sides by yarn that has been whipped over the edges through holes punched with a paper punch. Tabs were hand stitched to the top (see page 19 for instructions on making these tabs), and the mola hung on a rod.

The tote bag in Illus. 41 is decorated with a simple mola. To make one like it, first cut out the pieces, following Illus. 100, and enlarging the pattern as much as you wish. You need four pieces: the bag's front and back, and the front and back lining. Draw a pattern of a butterfly following Illus. 41 (you can trace the design right from the color picture), or whatever design you want. Then transfer the pattern to the front of the bag and cut it out.

Sew the lining to the front, wrong sides together. Turn under and hem the edges of the butterfly, thereby creating the reverse appliqué effect on the bag's front. Then sew the lining to the back of the bag, again with the wrong sides together.

Now, with the *right* sides of the bag together, stitch, by machine or by hand, the lined front and back together, leaving a small section of the bottom open so that you will be able to turn the bag. Press the seams flat, notch the corners and turn the bag right-side-out. Hand stitch the opening. The bag is complete.

This book has introduced you to a variety of appliqué techniques. You should now have enough know-how to create many appliqué projects.

Index

CREDITS

Illus. 36 by Larry Bauers; Illus. 8, 12, 13, 17, 37, 39, 79, 90 by Marion Beiker; Illus. 21, 23, 32, 41, 92, 94, 95, 96, 99 by Marcus Dillon, Jr.; Illus. 29, 30, 58 by Paul Miracle; Illus. 1, 2, 3, 5, 6, 7, 28, 30, 31, 34, 35, 38, 40, 45, 47, 60, 63, 65 by Dave Regier; Illus. 46 by Jo Christensen.

The authors would like to thank the following people, without whose help this book could not have been possible: Lisa Ashner, Stuart Ashner, Joy Bauers, Jackie Beaty, Marion Beiker, Gloria Berenson, Betty Christensen, Cynthia Ferrell, Irene Ferrell, John Ferrell, Sharon Hanlon, Luciano Ippolito, Jean Rae Lorie, Carolyn Lorrin, Roxanne Powell, Anna Lee Rublin, Terry Thompson, Marie Vance, and Carolyn Yates.

Thanks also to the personnel of two elementary schools in Shawnee Mission, Kansas: Rushton Grade School's principal, Charles H. Smith; Grace Williamson and her first-second graders; and Judy Nagel and her sixth graders; Dorothy Moody School's principal Kenneth L. Locke; Karen Gast and her third graders; Elyse Roberts and her fourth graders; and Kala Musick and her fifth graders.

The authors also thank Sonie Ashner's mother and partner in Morningside Knit Shop, Kansas City, Missouri, Mrs. Dorothy Shapiro Amdur, for inspiration.